HOW TO
BE BOZz

A guide to sucksess

for new bugs

by

alexander

de pfefel-jonson

For everyone who
would never
ever vote Tory

Contents

7 .... Back to skool agane

8 .... St. cnut's explained

8 .... Cads, oiks and goodie-goodies
and how to spot them

12 .... How to use lat. to make people
think you hav a big brane

14 .... Seens from history

15 .... Sum gurls i hav met

16 .... The patented de-pfefel jonson
excus-o-matik

18 .... Hard werk (and how to avoide it)

20 .... How to be whiz at games

22 .... Europ

26 .... Half turm report

28 .... Wokhampton prep.

30 .... The two tipes of spekers

32 .... How i got Tuxxit dun

36 .... Bulingdon club for super ace bois

38 .... How to fule the meedia

40 .... On the campane trale

42 .... Menewile in dorm no. 10

44 .... End of turm

BACK TO SKOOL AGANE

Hello fokes. It's me e.g. alexander de-pfefel jonson the curse of st. cnuts and once and futur world king.

This book wil teech you How to sukseed, how to leed and how to be topp.

All bois from st. cnuts end up with super topp jobs as any fule kno and liv lifes of top jolly japes becos we are the best so our maters and paters sa.

If you reed this book you will find out how YOU can one da become as grate and powerful as me and go on to hold TOP JOBS in briton like gov. of the bank of ingland, hed of the bbc. or editor of the daley tellegraf. (You will not acheev this if you do not atend st. cnut's skool for bois I am afrade tho so giv up now and do not bother trying)

St. Cnut's Explaned

A piktorial education for new bugs

This is me and my grate frend camron which means we tuouogh each other up continually. We argue a lot saying am not am am not am not ect. He is a grate frend, even tho he hav a face like a boild ham har har oink oink.

Together we batle aganst our comon enemis e.g. the masters chizz chizz. This is wut make us ante establishmunt. This put us in a grate posishon to be leders of men. We no wut it is like to sufer opression and hav to do without when the tuk shop run out of lemon drops on a thursda boo boo.

One da soon me or camron wil be hed boi of st. cnut's. It is our manifest destine. Our raisin detr. We wer born to rool and nothing wil stand in our wa.

i sa i wil always suport camron if he become hed boi befor me but in realite i wil stop at nothing untill i am topp of the skool. I skeme and plot and wil not rest untill i get wut i want. Apart from on sundas and just after prep. A groing boi need his rest as any fule kno.

But for now i wil pla the part of the grate frend to his big pink boild ham face and conspir with camron to bring down the masters and hav oven reddy tuk for al bois.

Apart from weedy gov jr. He is a weed and can do won.

The bois at st. cnut's ar encourajed to
develop interpursonal skils

CADS, OIKS AND GOODY-GOODIES AND HOW TO SPOT THEM

1.

Jakub rees mog
is a big gurl who
miss his nany
and cry at nite.
He think he liv in
eduardian tims
and dres lik an
undertaker. He
think he is v. clev
and talk lik this:
fwar fwar fwar.

2.

rishmal richbanks is head of the skool
and captane of everything and winer of
the mrs infosis prize for rafia work. Even
tho he much smaller than me his pater is
very rich and hav a super rolls enuff said.

3.

Hullo clouds, hullo human rites, hullo law. Here come flip flop fop keer fotherington-stamer and he is wok af.

He say he care about people with les than us and we should all pick flowers and mak daisy chanes. Chizz chizz lolle.

Let me add my strength to yores

HOW TO USE LAT. TO MAKE PEOPLE THINK YOU HAV A BIG BRANE

It is easy to go thru skool and not lern a thing about the reel werld. This is why lat. is good.

I sit in lat. class making ink blot pictures of busses ful of smiling hapy people while lat. master drone on bla bla bla dominus dominos deliverus deliveroo ect. ect.

But lat. can be useful. You can sa thing lik monerer moneresis moneratur as any fule kno and people think you v. clev indede.

My advise to anyone who want to sukcseed is to lern one lat. phrase and use it whenever pos.

If someone ask you if you make a mess in the dorm just say 'non tali auxilio nec defensoribus istis tempus eget' and run awa quickly saying chizz chizz. The prols will think you v. clev wise and strong and mak you leder in no time.

Gov jr. is so wok and metero thes dais that he think dubble lat. is a fancy cofe order in the tuk shop. But it not. Dubble lat. is frankli to much lat. imhoe chizz chizz.

In dubble lat. mi mind wonders and I dreem of riting ekselent plays (like mi hero shakspere who i wil finish mi disertation about one da) and performing them to clas SW1a and all the lat. masters.

Wen mi play finish, the bois wil chere and sa de-pfefel jonson yu are the gratest riter in the hole history of st. cnut's!

They wil cary me on thare sholders and treet me lik a romen emperror. i wil get a buk deel and go to south of frans.

My latin pla

Scene one: a vila in rome
Enter marcus aurelius de-pfefel jonson

Marcus: Eheu!

(The headmaster and all lat. masters who watch think this is a grate joke and ror with larffter)

Roman legionnare: i arrest you marcus aurelius for braking lokdown lors and holding a debauched orgi in the coliseum while the peepl sufered outside in the plag.

Marcus: But keer fotherington-stamer drink a ginjer beer and eet a forrin meal!

Roman legionnaire: But that not against the lor?

Marcus: Eheu! Chizz chizz!

(he run awa to spane)
(Headmaster and all lat. masters larff agane)

SEENS FROM HISTORY

The mitey cincinatus de-pfeffel jonson return to his plow
after saving roam from invashon by terribul hords.
Proving he is A TRU LEADER among men.

SUM GURLS I HAV MET

Even tho st cnut's is historicle jus for bois, sadly there are tims you ma have to come in contact with sum gurls. Heer are sum gerls i have met yuk yuk ect. ect.

Mad lissy lettis
She is mad. Some time she sa the madest things. Like she will save the werld. But she wil not. She is a disgrayce chizz chizz pork pork.

Wobbli therese
she lik to sa i am strong and staybl al the time but she is week and wobbli and i will destroi her one da. She was caught by matron running thru the weet fields and hav to leeve.

Maggi
Used to be the hed gurl and very scarey lik a dragen. My grate frend camron always sa he luv her and i larff and sa he wet.

princess nut nuts
i sometimes feel funy around her but she shouted at me and tel me to "get of her laptop" so i thump her and pull her pigtales

THE PATENTED DE-PFEFEL JONSON EXCUS-O-MATIK

It is eesy – and a grate plan – to go thru lif taking as litel responsibilite as pos. (and as much cred). But some time a master may catch you sherking at skool and sa "You boi, wut yu think yu are doing?"

At this point it is alwas gud to hav an excus redy. This is wen the patented de-pfefel jonson excus-o-matik (2/- from grabers) come in handy. Close your eys, pok it with a pensil and sa the first thing yu see. If you ar bold enuff and stik to yore storey thay wil beleev you. Hurrah!

(Apart from su gray who is a roten swot and a prig who love the rools chizz chizz boo)

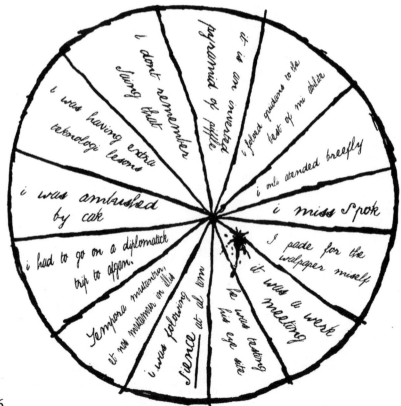

Ambushed by cak agane!

HARD WERK IS IMPORTENT
(but knoing how to avoide it is genius)

Roam was not bilt in a da. Obvs. It is masiv and a da is v. short as any fule kno. But statment stil stand. If you want something, you must werk hard for it. Or at lest get others to werk hard for it.

Hard werk is supposed to be GOOD FOR YOU. Every master, hed, and wel-mening aunt will tell you so until blu in the face. But in practis, dere reder, it is not as esy as it sounds. When faced with the chois betwene hard werk and absoluteli anything els, absoluteli anything els wil win out every tim. This is a perfectly natural instinckt, lik avoiding exersise or finding a hiding place when matron approach with a big thermom.

Cobra metings
These are not as exiting as thay sound. Thay do not involv acktual liv cobras. Or any snak at al. Thay are meerly another oportunity to sit bord in another clas whil people say Ver Important Things, non of wich involv eeting chese or having fun in ani wa.

Chese, unlike hard werk, provid imediate comfort and satisfacshon. With chese, dere reder, yore reward is instant. It is an indulgence that is holey its own excuse.

Someone hav to enjoi the gud things in life. To remind us al why we werk so hard in the first plase. Who better to mak that sacrifise than me? If I wer at every meteing, there would be no tim left to lift the skool spirit with a smile, a jape, or a quot from Lat. No time to experiens the veri things that we fite to protect (stilten, cheder, bree ect. ect.)

Hard werk may bild caracter, but it is chese that feed the sole.

How to avoide werk alltogether
REPONISBILITE is a terible pane chizz chizz. (Imagin having a bebe? Not likly. *Shuder!*) The most important thing to no about how to avoide werk is to alwas be sene to be doing *something*. Be shore to use long werds, wav hands a lot and – as alwas – do not be afrade to use Lat. if necessare.

DELEGASHUN is yore freind. Use phrase like "I hav ful confidens in gov. jr. to tak the ranes on this one" or "gov. jr. is exactli the rite boi for this job" even tho gov. jr. is obvs an oili oik and clerely not the rite boi for ani job at al! har har!

Another useful tacktick is MISS DIRECSHON. If someone sa "ware were you in that geog. leson?" yu sa "Ah, yes, geog. But wut we realy shud be talking about is the need to keep are spirits up at this difacult tim! That why I've been tirlesly werking on a new inishtive to suport local chese makers...." By the tim they realiz what happen, you can be alreddy half way to a picknic.

Ded cats

If al els fale, and responsibilite bare down on yu lik a frate trane, do not be scared to use ACTUAL CHESE as a decoi. Arange to be photo'd with a big weel of stilten and sa it represent the resiliens of the bois of st. cnut's. Befor yu no it peeple wil be talking about the importans of local chese prod and not about how yu mised yet another cobra meteing.

Sum plases to hide when yore suposed to be werking

HOW TO BE WIZZ AT GAMES

1. Rugger

3. Criket

2. Foopball

4. Wif-waf

EUROP. IS IT JUST A BIG CHIZZZ?

As you ma hav gessed fokes, Geog. (Lik mani other lesons)
is not a partickular strong point of min. You wud be rite.
I do tend to doz of in geog. lesons and dreme that i am
steping up to the crese at lords to face the final ball of the
ashs… with jus six runs needed for victory the croud holds
its breath as the mitey topp batsman de pfeffel-jonson
get redy to smash the wining shot into the stands… but i
dygress…So why wud i be intrested in wether we shud be a
part of europ or not? I wil explane…

The bois of st. cnut's (who ar v. werld-wise and traveled as
any fule kno) are biterly devided on this mattr. It is a debat witch
threten to tare the skool a part. Shud we be in europ or shud we
go it allone? The mitey britania rooling the wavs once agane?

Some sa we should be a part of bigest trad blok in the
hole werld. That the chans to liv and work in frans germ. it.
holend ect. ect. far outways ani conserns we may hav about
loosing culchure or heritag.

They sa that the sun alwas shinning and the uplands are
filed with beatifull flours.* That in thees modern tims we shud
be a part of sum kind of thrusting dinamic europian onion.

Menewile other bois sa if we in europ we wil loose our
sovrinty and our mony and end up rooled by unelected
bizybode bods in brustles (chizz chizz sprouts!).

One such boi is nijel farash in yr. 8. He is a v. od caracter
indede. He sa he hats europ but he tend to ware laderhosen
and stomp about the plase singing old germen songs.

But farash is v. popler among a sertain tipe of boi in the
skool. Thay sa he is a man of the peple and sa it lik it is (even tho
his pater is v. rich and own a bank or sumthing.) This of corse,
dere reder, cud put a dent in my plan to becum hed boi of st.
cnut's, then prim. min. then ultimatle werld king. If thay vot for

---

*This ma sound like the sort of thing weedie sop flip-flop wok fop keer fotherington-stamer
wood sa - but apparentle he think we ar better off out of europ now. Whatevs.

him then i ma never get the topp job i so richli deserv.

Sum of the bois in form SW1a sa thay agree with nijel farash. Rees-mog sa if we ar part of europ then we cant use ofshore banks and that are maters and paters wud loose an abs forchune. This cud severly afect mi tuk money going forwerd. Let alon chrismus presents … this is obvs a big consurn. Chizz chizz big prob.

So it not reley a question of wether i think we shud be in or out of europ, but wich posishun wil mak me mor popler?

I have writen two lists too help me mak mi mind up:

PROS AND CONS OF EUROP

PROS	CONS
Chese	Strate banans
Pritier gurls	Standerdised sausij at Brek.
Beter at sports	The metric sistem (wut the hec is a Kelo?)
Beter motor cars	Money (thay want to BAN the Brit shilling)
quossants	Everything is in french
ice creme	~~Beaurocrats~~ ~~Bueaucrats~~ ~~Benrocrats~~
	Rude wayters.

I wil tak my tim and conside my posishun carfuly befor i decid. The futur prospecks for bois of st. cnut's (and also – to a leser extent – the rest of briton obvs) is an enormus consurn. But the futur prospecks for me - alexander de-pfefel jonson - must alwas tak presedent…

Desishions desishions…

"The sunlit uplands awate us!"

ST. CNUT'S

HALF TURM REPORT

NAME: alexander de pfeffel jonson

FORM: sw1a

SUBJECT	GRADE	REMARKS
Hist.	D-	This boy seems to think the purpose of history is to remember him.
Geog.	D	Some of Johnson's dated comments about other countries are unacceptable in the modern age.
Eng.	F	Claims Shakespeare is his hero, but is yet to submit his final dissertation on the subject. The endless excuses for failure to deliver are becoming tiresome.

Lat.	*D+*	Has adopted a disgracefully cavalier attitude to his classical studies. I will be surprised if this boy ever remembers one Latin phrase correctly.
Games	*E*	Thinks the rules of the games do not apply to him.
Technol.	*F*	Seems to have an inability to find crucial files, saying they have been deleted. Seemed to perk up when I mentioned he could do with extra technology lessons...

HEADMASTER'S COMMENTS

Johnson sometimes seems affronted when criticised for what amounts to a gross failure of responsibility - and surprised at the same time that he was not appointed Captain of the school for the next half. I think he honestly believes that it is churlish of us not to regard him as an exception, one who should be free of the network of obligation that binds everyone else.

Wokhampton prep.

The skool ware you can get expeld just for saing you are brit boo chizz!

As yu are aware bi now, st. cnut's is the best skool and produce the gratest bois who go on to be captens of industri, general heros and roolers of men. On other sid of the vilage however is wokhampton prep. boo boo chizz chizz.

They ar wok af. In fac thay ar so wok thay let in skolarship bois AND gurls. (it like thay do not even no wut a gurl is).

Thay sa that at wokhampton prep. you are kept in stone cells underground and fed nothing but grool. All the lessons ar about how to use pronuns. Lessons go on for 25 hours a day, and if you get your pronuns wrong they lock you in a dark cupboard with rats. Its true. Yar boo suks.

*****

Bois in wokhampton prep. are not like bois in fab st. cnut's. Insted of saing "You uterly wet weed!" "You grate big gurl's blouse!" or "You naddering skool swot!" thay sa "O i am sori did i ofend yu?"

Wokhampton prep. hed boi jereme corbine sa everybode should hav wirless in there dorm – payd for by the skool. This is comunism and hav no place in A MODERN SKOOL. He is a Mutton-headed old mugwump and should go back to izlington and eat avocardo with the lesbines. Chizz chizz!

*****

Another big diference between st. cnut's and wokhampton prep. is obvs the gurls. But thay are not prity quiete gurls who wood not say boo to a goos, but loud and noisie and not at all ladelik . . . . .

Angeler ranner is hed prefect and hav a vois lik a foghorn. A proper teror who always think she is rite. She strut about like she is the kween. Only at wokhampton prep. can a girl be hed prefect boo boo. This wil never hapen at st. cnut's where we no only bois can keep a level hed wen tims ar tuouogh.

Thare ar other gurls as wel lik dian abot who is a bolshi
rev. who sa tuk money is capitalist conspirsy. She would prob.
hav us all ware hemp uniform and plant veg. in the quad

She wag her finger and sa "yu cant sa that any more yu'll
get throne in gale" but she strugle with basic algeb. and math.
We tees her about this al the tim. "YU CANT DO SUMS
CHIZZ CHIZZ"

*****

They hav SEVEN BINS in evry dorm and insted of chapl
thay hav a *saf space* where thay can even pray to ala, buda or
whatevs. Everything is a 'ishue' and nobody get detensh cos
punishment is opreshon.

All the tuk in there tuk shop is mad from veg. and taste
like the insid of gov. jr's plimpsoles. Thay want al skools to be
powerd by winmils and motor cars to run on potatoe.

Thay sa the wokhampton prep. wa is mor fare and we
shud let them hav a go. But it is onli the bois from st. cnut's
who hav the necessare wisdom and natural abilite to lede
as any fule kno.

THE TWO TIPES OF SPEKERS

The speker of the debating soc. at skool's job is to say: "Order! Order! Stop chuntering from a sedentary posishon de-pfefel jonson and let the others hav a sa!" He even mor importent than blak rod… (shut up camron larffing…)

The speker sit in his chare lik he is a judg and the bois al pretend to care – when reley we ar just wating to go to lunch and hav extra sossig and mash befor it run out.

But it is an important roll. He sa "let yore onorable grate frend fotherinton-stamer speke mr. jonson!" (even tho he is obvs not reley my freind) and genrally keep the piece. There are two tipes of speker as the tittel at the top of this pag sa.

1. The meannie

This tipe of speker is the wurst. He wont let me get awa with anething. Wen i tri to prorog the deb. societey or lie to the matron in order to push Tuxxit thru he sa "I do not giv a flying flamingoe" and that it is aganest the rools. Boo chizz chizz

2. The cissie

This is much beter and easier to control. He sa order order - sam as a meannie - but yu can tel his hart not in it. Yu can get whatevs you want with this tipe of chap and long ma he rain. He sa he is imparshall but he alwas let me sa more wenever we debate aganste wokhampton prep. He sa if you do not stop i wil hav to arsk you to stop agane…Cheers cheers!

How i got Tuxxit dun

Thru al the hist. of st. cnut's tuk shop, the stok has alwas bin suplied by grabers confecshon trading emporium ltd. A nasty gruby litle bonne-bonne compane run by a dark harey man who look distinckly forrin to me.

Sum of the bois hav alwas argud that this control ove our lemon drops and sherbut fountens by unelected bizzybodes hold us bak. That if we seezed controle of the suppli of tuk to the shop it wud mak us stronger and put us in a posishun to bild opertunites for trad with exiting new markits such as wokhampton prep. and skools in other far awa villeges.

My grate frend camron sa we shud hav a ref. on wether to remane or leev the curent tuk arangement in the deb. soc. and that the desishun shud be binding. Sum how he got the masters to agree to it and the rest is hist. Camron may be a wurthles sniveling wede with a face like a boild ham but he wil alwas be rememberd for this.

Now being an ambishus sort of a chap and as part of my on-going plan to becom hed boi of st. cnut's and ultimatle werld king i seezed upon this as a grate chans to grab vots from eesily swaid bois in years 1 and 2. At furst my atempts to win bois ove was faling on def ears… That was untill i met the weerdo missfit with od skils that go bi the nam of domnick sigismund arbuthnot cuming.

Dom. tak the ranes of my campane. He sa the bes wa to convins bois to leve the tuk union is to tel lyes. To me - who hav not a shred of desency in my bode - this seme fare enuff.

He invent jenius phras:

TAK BAK CONTROL OF OUR TUK

- wich not reley mak sens but sound grate - and help convins the bois that if we remane with grabers then hordes of van drivers from places lik turkeye wil invade the halowed hals of st. cnut's taking jobs of desent brit truk drivers.

Dom cuming crepes around the skool grounds

Obvs i do not giv a fig about brit truk drivers but it sound lik a vot winer. Cheers cheers!

Cuming also hav grate ide that in sted of posters and bils on skool wals ware everybode cud se them, we shud rite speshul nots with individuale taylored lyes on them and put them in each bois pigin hols. Lik "vot leve or it wil be dubble lat. evry thurs. for specifickally you!" This is ver smart and analitickal and not aganest the rools in ane wa as any fule kno…

He also think up the jenius grate big lye:

WE GIV £3/5/− TO GRABERS EVRY WEDS − LETS GIV IT TO MATRON INSTED

The bois lov this even tho thay do not partikularly care a buton about matron as all descent bois at st. cnut's hav privat doc's at hom anywa.

Dom sa this wil help....

I kno we do not hav a plan in plas for the suppli of lemon drops from ire. for exampl but dom sa not to worri about it. It is beter if we do not acktually win, jus get a lot of vots that send a messag to the bois about how powerfull i am and that wil help my chanses of being hed boi at the next elecshun.

The da of the big ref. arive and

GET TUXXIT DUN

is the phras on everybodes lips as we nervusly wate for the risult…

We won. Get ove it.

It is 52 pla 48 wich is a resounding victore as any fule kno.

Now, 8 munths later the tuk shop is in a terible stat. There are no lemon drops du to on going situashun with supliers in ire. (that nobode cud hav forsene) and their is nobode to man the tuk shop on tues. and wed. The van driver went bak to turkeye and thay hav not been abel to find a replasement prepard to werk for the pitence grabers wer paing him.

We sa it is cos Tuxxit was not dun propperly. That bois lik flip flop wok fop met lib keer fotherington-pronun-hapy-elit-stamer (chizz chizz) wer frustrating it at evry singel oppertunity. The bois swalow the lye hole and rees-mog sa thay jus hav to beleev harder. This agane mak no sens but seme to werk!

Dom disapere. Thay sa he was las sene driving of in a motor car to a nereby cassle.

But i do not care. I hav a privat suppli of lemon drops sent to me eech month by mater and pater anywa so it not efect me one jot hurrah!

The crushal thing is that the hole afare mad everybode talk about what is the mos impotant thing here. Me. alexander de-pfefel jonson. And frankli stuf the tuk shop. Chizz chizz. Mor sherbut anybode? Not you gov. jr, yu hav had enuff…

THE BULINGDON CLUB FOR SUPER ACE BOIS

Thare ar meny socs. at st. cnut's such as debating soc. nat. hist. soc. drama soc. ect. ect. These are manely just an excus for swots to sho of in front of the masters. Look at me sir i no al the kings and kweens in the rite order and hav mad up a song about it for you sir.

Meenwhile i, the grate alexander de-pfefel jonson, want no part of this and onli hav tim for one soc. The gratest soc. of them al. Counting barrons, princes, earls and chancelers of the exchecker as its parst members, its the one and only Bulingdon soc. CHEERS CHEERS!

Can yu think of any other soc. ware yu can go out to a super spiff restrant, smash the plas up then strole of as if nuthing hapened? Wel that is wut the bois of the bulingdon do. And al yu hav to do to be a member is burn a 10/- note in front of a prol on the st.

Evryone lov a bit of bulingdon

Here we ar puling our touoghest faces and looking reley quit spiffing

Being part of bulingdon soc. is ace. You get yor one speshul costum wich look supercool and we al stand on the steps looking lik gansters for a foto.

Oo er coo lumme look at them...

Then we charge ta-ran-ta-ra ta-ra

WAM BIFF ur-ur-ur.

The restarant is distroyed. The restarant owners ar devestated.

Flip-flop wok fotherington-imigrant-frendly-stamer sa gosh do you think you should be doing that, de-pfefel jonson, is it kind? To which I repli if i had a germ gun i would blast them with 5 trilion bakterial volts so they are getting off litely.

I arsk yu? Wut is the point of being filthi rich if you cant lord it ove the prols once in a wile?

How to ~~fule~~ deel with the meedia

If, lik me, yu ar wel on yore wa to being werld king, yu wil need to hav a plan for how to deel with the inevitabl meedia attenshun. Peeple wil want to kno wut yu are up too wether yu lik it or not so yor public profil wil hav to be managd v. carfully (it not lik yu can jus tel them the truth for heven sake…)

Here ar mi tips for how to absolutle ace it as a modern meedia personalite/politishun ….

1. Tradishunal broadcast meedia

Lora k. is cheef politikal reporter for st. cnut's broadcasting corpuration. Lukily she is grate frends with nanny and think i am the bees nees. Not lik nasti beth riggers from rival skye who alwas sa "but that is a lye pfefel-jonson, dont yu owe it to the bois of st. cnut's to tel the truth?" and iritating things lik that. Lora is prepard to jus repete evrything i sa without question lik a GUD JURNALIST. Befor i mete lora i alwas scruf up mi hare a bit to mak me seme mor of a cheekie chappie.

2. Podcarsters

This is a modurn phenom. A bit lik ham radio. Two
(normully) men sit in a dark rum and talk lik they ar in
a public hous. Bla bla bla i think jonson shud do this no
i think he shud do that. But unlike offishul st. cnut's
meedia they use fack chekers and do not nede to aply
balans so best AVOIDE AT AL COSTS imhoe….

3. The rags

Choos who you speke to wisely. It is fin to speke to the skool
papes, but steer clere of leftie rags lik the gaurdine chizz chizz…

This is me campaneing ruthlesly

ON THE CAMPANE TRALE

As chrismuss approach (hurrah!) mi campane to becom hed
boi of st. cnut's begins in ernest. i pul out al the stops.

Furst i present my manefesto.

Mi Manefesto

by alexander de-pfefel jonson

Recrut 20,000 new prefects

Bild 40 new sick rooms for matron

"australian-style" house point sistem

Increase nationl living poket money rate

generic "leveling up"*

unicorns probably?

*leveling up is a particularle grate phras as it mene abs. nothing!

Sure it is a littel lite on detale but it is nerely chrismuss
as i sa so the bois jus want to see a happy face and not sum
miserry guts teling them the truth chizz chizz... Vot for the
boi who got Tuxxit done hurrah! Sure, its not as oven reddy
as we promised but we hav taken bak control of the lunch
que. Wel, at leste in the sens that sum of us can push to the
front of it noe...

After hiding in the tuk shop fridge (a tactical masterstrock
if i sa so miself) to avoid awks questons from the hed prefect
about the continued problem of the mising lemon drops, i
am wa ahed in the poles and things are looking up for me
and - to a leser extent - grate briton! Hurrah hurrah!

MENEWILE IN DORM NO. 10

"It was a werk event. All gidence was follode."

End of turm

The last weeks of skool turm are full of super wheezes japes and pranks. Cheers cheers! We hav bin pumped brim full of knolege for wekes on end and the tim to let our hare down has finely arived.

Mi grate freind Camron smugle bootles of BEER and cakes into the dorm room in a sootcase when suposed to be loked down. Midnite feasts and pillow fights for al. Whiz whiz!

Sum of the youngr bois are sik on the carpit and a swing gets brok in the quad but nobodi care as we ar in demob mode and nuthing can stop us. We ar the bois of st. cnut's and this is are tim.

Flip flop wok keer fotherington stamer - hullo clouds, hullo lesbines, hullo non bineries - tri to spoil our fun and tel matron. But we deni evrything and sa we were folowing gidelines at al tims. We get away scot free hoora!

Thay sa that there wil be an investigashun in du corse. i sa i wil abid by the result of the investigashun (but i hav my fingers crosed behind my bak har har).

People hav short memries. Thay wil onli remember the gud tims and the japes and the Lat. quots and not the rool braking and the constant lyeing.

Befor to long mater and pater arrive to tak me away for the holidays. We ar off to Russha agane. i wav goodbi from the back of the car as we drive up the gravl path of st. cnuts at the end of another hard turm.

But - lik cincinatus - i wil return . . . .

"1957 is going to be grate fokes..."

This buk could not have been made without the folowing people who are al super top spiffing chaps as any fule kno!

Mat Morrisroe, Richard Howe, Darren (a wet and a weed), Phil Lovell, Alfred Armstrong, Andy OBrain, Peter Mathers, Crippen of Claygate, Lesley Scarles, Cis Heaviside, Pete Paphides, Will Watkinson, Tom Saunders, Scott Millar, Crab, Sharon Rossiter, Catherine RW, Helen Kemp, Gemma Ball ov corse, Caroline Gerrard, Jane Trobridge, Barnsley Sime, Jon Canning, Dancing Gardener, Cosmic Kakapo, Rufus Hound, Sean M Thompson, Joël Lacey,

Alistair Coleman, Martin Brazier, Steve Potz-Rayner, Rob Jones, Neil, Paul Westerman, Steve Mainprize, Alan McGlennan, Jeerrrmy Stepehens, Brian Edwards, Jim Mortleman, Dave Williams, Paul Edwards, Stuart Fraser, Jerry Quartley, James Docherty and gurningchimp

Cheers cheers!

about the riter

Chris Barker is an art director, artist and general tomfoolerer who is possibly best known for his annual Sgt. Pepper dead celebrity montages, the art-meets-light-entertainment book Brush Strokes, and the Tory election wipeout bingo cards from the 2024 election.

This book was an idea he had when he got up at 4am to go to the toilet (because he's that old now). It came to him in one big burst of inspiration so he wrote some notes on his phone before he forgot it (would recommend).

He looked at it again in the morning and – incredibly – still thought it was a funny idea so he made a couple of images of it and posted them online. More people than he had expected seemed to like it and tried to convince him it would be a good idea to do a whole book of the joke (he didn't take much convincing). There appears to be an underground subculture of Molesworth fans that the rest of the world is unaware of (altho any fule kno).

Chris has this terrible habit of looking at things and saying to himself "Yeah, I can see what they've done there… I could probably do that" but wants the rest of the world to know that trying to draw in the style of one of the greatest cartoonists – nay artists – of all time is absolutely nowhere near as easy as he had assumed it would be. Massive respect to Ronald Searle and Geoffrey Willans. You make it look reeley eesy.

Finally, the author would like you to know that he is aware that other books about Boris Johnson are available but this one is significantly shorter and has more pics. It's short because the joke isn't THAT funny. IS HE?

HUGE special thanks to
Adrian Barker, Richard Tingley and Lewis Barker
for their artistic contribs (pgs 17,19, 20, 24, 42)
and to Dan Sumption at Peakrill Press for pub.ing